Beacon Hill P
Kansas

ING
RIND

D0424426

Copyright 2004
by Cecil Murphey and Beacon Hill Press of Kansas City

ISBN 083-412-1344

Printed in the
United States of America

Cover Design: Ted Ferguson

Library of Congress Cataloging-in-Publication Data

Murphey, Cecil B.
    [Breaking the silence]
    When someone you love suffers from depression or mental illness : daily
encouragement / Cecil Murphey.
        p. cm.
    Originally published: Breaking the silence. Louisville, Ky. : Westminster/
John Knox Press, c1989.
    Includes bibliographical references.
    ISBN 0-8341-2134-4 (pbk.)
    1. Mentally ill—Family relationships—Prayer-books and devotions—English.
I. Title.

    BV4908.5.M85 2004

                                                        2004016233

10   9   8   7   6   5   4   3   2   1

CONTENTS

First
Focus

"If Only I Had..."

"We all react differently to pressure," the caseworker assured me. "He turned the pressure inward, and that led to his depression."

More than once I heard the comforting words that tried to assure me I had done nothing wrong. Yet I thought, *If only I had noticed his behavior earlier. If only I had insisted he see a doctor. If only I had been kinder and more sensitive.* Logic told me that my earlier awareness would not have made much overall difference and that going over the what-if facts now wouldn't help. Yet my emotions still churned.

The caseworker suggested I reverse the what-if approach by asking, *What if I had forever ignored his problem? What if I had refused to get help for him? What if I hadn't cared?* Those answers have helped to make his situation easier for me to accept.

God, deliver me from my torturous questions, and remind me that I did the best I knew how. With Your help, I'm going to be more sensitive to his needs.

7

Demanding Love

God, if she would get even a little better, I'd be encouraged. She got worse. I became more demanding in my prayers and, I suspect, more demanding of her. She got still worse.

One day when she was lucid, she said, "You don't love me, and I'm sorry I have to put you through this. I wish I'd die; it would be easier for everybody."

I hurriedly assured her that I loved her and didn't want her to die. Afterward I probed my heart. *Do I love her? Yes,* I answered, *I do.*

Why couldn't she believe I loved her? I knew why: my kind of love made demands. I offered a love with conditions tied to it: *Get better, and you'll get more love.*

I'm slowly changing. I began by saying, "I love you. I'll always be here for you, no matter how you behave."

Did she improve after that? Or did my change make it seem that way? She *is* better now—and so am I.

God, because You accepted me, I'm learning to accept her exactly as she is now. Thank You.

Sick Denials

May my cry come before you, O LORD; give me understanding according to your word (Ps. 119:169).

He was only 14 the first time he said, "I think I'm crazy or something."

"Everybody feels like that at times," I said.

For the next three years my son tried to tell me in different ways that he was mentally ill, but I refused to hear and instead resorted to quick words of reassurance: "You'll grow out of this."

I played the game of denial. I couldn't believe that *my* wonderful child needed psychiatric treatment.

When the school counselor said, "He has serious problems and needs help," I finally stopped my denial.

Lord, forgive me for ignoring the truth. Help me to listen to his cries of pain no matter how much I don't want to hear. I desperately need Your strength and understanding.

You Don't Need to Be Here

The doctor explained my wife's diagnosis and told me the name of the medicine they were giving her. When I asked about getting her out of the hospital, he said, "We'll have to talk about that later."

"But she's not sick—not *really* sick," I said.

"She's *very* sick," he said emphatically.

When I saw my wife, I said, "I know you've been under a strain, and you're high-strung, but you don't need to be here—not like all these sick people."

"I *do* need to be here," she said. "I'm as sick as any of the others."

After several long talks with her doctor, I stopped denying that she was deeply depressed and that she was getting worse.

Now, four months later, I'm glad the doctor insisted. She's better. They were both right: she needed to be there.

God, help me to accept her needs and to stop trying to deny her illness.

Unheard Cries

I went through a night of torment. When I arrived home earlier than expected, I found his suicide note, which read, "I can't take it anymore." I called the paramedics, and they rushed him to the hospital in time. I sat all night in the room with him and asked myself questions.

Why? Did I fail him? These things don't just happen. My son must have been troubled a long time and I didn't know—or didn't want to know.

Looking back, I recalled examples of bizarre behavior. He had been trying to tell me for a long time—through cries I didn't hear, such as his odd behavior and confused conversation. I turned deaf until he broke through the silence in the only way he knew how.

Lord, thank You that he's alive so that I can now listen. With Your help, I won't seal him into silence again. Thank You for giving me a second chance.

Admitting It

They called me *strong*. *Brave*. *Kind*. I loved hearing words like that. I put up with a husband who underwent psychiatric treatment in the hospital five times. I never complained. Everyone said I smiled in the face of adversity.

But I was presenting a beautiful facade, although I didn't realize it then. I persistently pushed away my own pain and gave the world a bright smile.

Last week his therapist talked to me and refused to allow me to lie to myself any longer. "You're hurting," he said. "He has embarrassed and angered you. Don't hold back—it's all right to admit it."

"Yes," I said through my tears. I had pushed the pain away and hidden the hurt from myself. Now I'm getting help in facing my true feelings.

Lord, I want to be caring and supportive. I need Your grace in my neediness so that I can help him with his problems.

Who's Sick?

I didn't know what her therapist would tell me to do, but I never expected what he did say: "Get help for yourself."

"Me?" I replied in shock. *"I'm* not the sick one. I haven't gone through terrible depressions and—"

"No," he said softly, "you're not sick. But you need help too." When I continued to balk, he said, "Look at it this way. The more help you get, the better you can cope with her. Furthermore, mental illness—or any other kind of illness—affects everyone in the family. If she had suffered a massive coronary and I suggested you attend a seminar, you wouldn't hesitate. So get help—immediately."

I did as he suggested. Besides seeing a therapist, I'm also getting help from a support group of families of mentally ill patients. I've learned a lot about her problem.

Lord, I'm glad I got help, because I'm stronger now. Thank You for showing me the way. Please show me now how to use my newfound strength in helping her.

Pull Yourself Out

God is our refuge and strength,
an ever-present help in trouble (Ps. 46:1).

I must have said to him 50 times, "If you'd make up your mind that you're OK, you could snap out of it."

One day his eyes filled with tears, and he said, "Do you think I *like* being this way, that I *choose* to be sick and a burden? If I had a broken leg, you wouldn't demand that I make up my mind to be well and then start walking."

The shock from those words made me face how cruelly I had spoken. He was sick and didn't have the choice of pulling himself together. I had been wrong; I apologized, and I've never said those words again.

Once I stopped demanding that he pull himself out of his problems, we began to work together. He's going to get better, and I'm with him all the way.

Dear Lord, thank You that the patient had the courage to tell the caregiver what she needed to hear. Give us both guidance as we struggle in this together.

Careful Words

I determined never to use words like *crazy* or *insane* around her. Mom had been through a lot in the past two years. Instead, I said, "When you were away," or "During your illness."

The rest of the family picked up my cue, and we chose our words so that we wouldn't remind her of her painful ordeal.

Once I laughingly said to my brother, "Oh, you're crazy." As soon as the words passed my lips, I felt terrible.

"Compared to me, he's fine," Mom said. "Back there I was so crazy I fought getting a shot because I thought you were paying them to kill me. Another patient laughed and said 'That's insane. Who would spend that much money to get rid of you?'"

Mom's freedom to say *crazy* and *insane* set us free from choosing our words so carefully.

God, we love Mom. Thank You that she has taught us that we can be ourselves around her—just the way we are around You.

Euphemisms

We couldn't face the shame of mental illness in our family, so we became experts at avoiding having to speak about it. We used words like "indisposed" or "convalescent."

If he's not normal, we secretly wondered, then what about the rest of us? What about our children? So we opted for nice words to disguise the horror of his situation.

When he came home for a weekend, I referred to his "resting" and his "trip." On the second day he screamed at me, "I'm sick! Sick! Sick! I'm a mental patient in a psychiatric hospital!"

He forced me to face the reality of his condition. Our using euphemisms—nice cover-up words—had enabled us to continue to deny the truth of his illness.

God, thank You for helping me to see that in some ways he's healthier than I am. He's mentally ill, and I need to recognize and call it by name as I continue to care for him.

How Long?

God [gives] endurance and encouragement (Rom. 15:5).

The doctor explained everything thoroughly, but I kept waiting for one answer. Finally I asked, "How long will he need treatment?"

"I have no way of knowing," she said. "Some people need medication their entire lives; others require drugs only periodically. I can't promise you an end to treatment. Our goal is to help the depressed and mentally ill achieve the highest degree of independence and productivity possible."

The words saddened me, although I knew she spoke honestly. I didn't get the answer I wanted, but I know that the medical profession, along with our network of friends, is with us in our day-to-day struggles.

Lord, I still cry out, "How long?" I want him well, and even though I don't see an immediate cure, hope still springs up, assuring me that one day he'll get better.

Cure?

Will she be cured? Ever? I think about this often. Her doctor avoids answering and says things like "She's improving" or "She'll adjust." Doesn't he hear my real question?

I want my wife *cured.* I don't want the threat of another attack hanging over our lives. If someone—anyone—would just say to me, "She's going to be cured," I could be at rest. But no one will say that. I suppose no one can guarantee the results. But *is* there no cure for depression and mental illness? Do they only adjust, cope, and improve? We get physically sick, and we recover. Why can't I know the same thing about depression and mental illness?

Finally I asked myself, *If I knew the answer, would it make a difference?* Whether she was sick or cured, I would still treat her lovingly. That's when I stopped asking the question.

God, I've demanded ultimate answers, and You keep trying to teach me to live in the immediate moment. Be patient with me; I'm learning.

For Whose Good?

I didn't tell our relatives about our son's problems. They all live out of state, and when they phoned I made excuses for his not being there. I think I covered it well. *I'm doing this for our son's good,* I told myself.

I told his doctor what I had done, and she assured me that many families go through this cover-up. "There are better ways of handling this," she said. She helped me to find a support group where I could talk about my needs. *And about him.*

One day I faced a hard fact. I hadn't withheld the truth for his good or for the relatives' protection. I did it because of my inability to admit how sick he was. Now the whole family knows. To my surprise, they've offered *me* as much support and comfort as they have him.

God, I was afraid for him—but just as much for myself. I still get afraid at times. Give me the strength and the courage I need to face each day.

Ashamed

*Cast all your anxiety on him
because he cares for you* (1 Pet. 5:7).

"You never talk about your wife," a coworker said. "You mention your children, your hobbies, but not your wife. Don't you get along?"

"We get along fine," I said and changed the subject. I was too ashamed to tell him that my wife is mentally ill. I didn't talk about her condition with anyone. I told our church friends she had gone to visit relatives "for a month or so."

Somehow our pastor found out she was in a psychiatric hospital, and he visited me. He said to me later, "It must be a heavy load that you're carrying—all by yourself. I wish you'd let us share your pain."

"I'm too ashamed," I said—the first time I had admitted that to myself. "Ashamed of what people will think. Of her. Of me. Ashamed of feeling this way."

"I can tell you only that *I* know about your wife, and I love you both," he told me.

God, thank You for someone who cares. His caring has helped me open up to others.

Mrs. Never-Wrong

"You're so absolutely perfect," said my sick son. "You have all the answers even when I don't have questions. You never make mistakes like the rest of us mortals. You're Mrs. Never-Wrong!"

His tirade went on and on, but I didn't hear anything after that. I had known for a long time how important it is for me to be right. Some of that came from my own childhood, where I felt I was never right. Yet it went deeper with me. I had trouble admitting mistakes. I didn't easily say, "I'm wrong and I'm sorry."

I've argued for hours with people, "proving" I was right. Now I'm becoming aware that to admit I'm wrong holds terror for me. I believed that to say I was wrong meant I had failed. I now know that if I fail in one incident, I haven't failed in everything. I finally learned to say, "I was wrong."

God of all knowledge, keep teaching me that I don't have to know everything. Help me see that only You are right 100 percent of the time.

Cop-Out

I've been struggling with my anger toward her for a long time. When things get tough, I have to fight. She cops out by checking into the mental ward. And that makes me really mad.

Why can't she carry her load? She lies in a hospital bed or walks around like a zombie while I hold down a job, try to take care of three children, and still visit her. Then I feel guilty for feeling this way. She didn't do this on purpose, and she didn't do it to make me mad.

I talked to our pastor, and she said, "I would feel the same way. It's normal to be angry at such behavior. Admitting your anger is the first step toward resolving the issue."

I still get frustrated with the load; I want her healthy. I wish life weren't working this way. But I'm learning to accept her way of trying to cope.

God of all emotions, help me to admit my feelings, no matter how negative they are. Make me healthy so I can help her on the way to health.

Death Wish

After months of deep inner turmoil, I finally said the words aloud in prayer: *I wish he would die!*

For a few minutes my imagination soared with the thoughts of the freedom and peace I would enjoy.

Then my feelings vacillated between guilt and desire. I had put up with him for so long that I was worn out. He had alienated our children. He had no friends left. I don't *really* want him to die. But once in a while, when the pressure gets heavy and he has an especially bad day, I think about his death.

In my support group, others told me they had similar fantasies. Knowing that I'm not the only one who has such moments helps me in my struggle with guilt feelings.

Omniscient God, You know my thoughts better than I do. Thank You for helping me accept my need to feel as I do.

Forgiving

Forgive whatever grievances you may have against one another (Col. 3:13).

I ought to forgive her. God tells me to; my friends and family say I must. She's begged me to forgive. "I want to," I said, "but I can't let go. You put me through too much pain just to forget it and go on as if it never happened."

I promised her I would try—and I did, but resentment and anger built up again. Today I figured out something: I have not truly wanted to forgive. I liked being angry and forcing her to try to please me. I'm ashamed of myself, but now that I understand myself better, I can let go. I don't have to hold on anymore.

Lord, You're always ready to forgive. I'm sorry it's taken me so long to want to wipe away all her mistakes. Help me to put away all the past hurts.

Responsible Limits

I wonder how often I grumbled about his not taking responsibility. I picked up and laundered his clothes, cleaned his room, cooked his meals. I grumbled about him whenever anyone asked how he was doing. I constantly felt exhausted doing everything for him.

Then a friend said, "People will be only as responsible as we let them."

"But if I didn't do all these things for him, they would never get done!"

"So what?" my friend said.

She helped me to face a harsh reality. I had limited his responsibility because he was not reliable. But then, he didn't have to be. The more I did for him, the more I hindered his progress.

Then I told him, "From now on, you're going to do things for yourself." He still doesn't take full responsibility, but he's getting better.

God, he's responsible to himself and to You. Don't let me forget that—ever.

The 49-Percent Rule

I'm the helper type, willing to do anything I can. Sometimes I do too much despite our doctor's warning—"Don't do too much for her."

Unfortunately, I found myself taking on more work, trying to make her life a little easier. For instance, on her worst days, I let her stay in bed and waited on her. Now I realize that had she gotten out of bed and done things for herself, she would have benefited.

Our doctor finally said, "Don't do more than 49 percent of any task. You can help, but she must learn to do things herself." Few things have caused me more trouble than holding to the 49-percent rule. I kept wanting to do just a little more. But I did insist she do things for herself. "If you have trouble, I'm here."

She's now much better. She's working part-time—a job she found by herself. I drive her to the bus line, and she goes the rest of the way alone.

Loving God, help me hold to the 49-percent rule—no matter how hard.

Expectations

"She's not getting any better," I said. After two years I resigned myself to the way things were.

When friends asked, "How's she doing?" my best answer was "About the same." To the question about progress, I shook my head. Six months ago a friend said, "As long as you're satisfied that she won't improve, she probably won't."

What a burden he had laid on me—as if I determined her condition! And yet I finally admitted, I did have something to do with progress.

Others who have mentally ill or depressed family members agreed with my friend. "You set the tone," one person said. "If you expect her to get better and help her, she does improve."

Since then I have been seeing slight signs of improvement. How much of it has come about because of my expectations?

God, I don't understand how my expectations affect her health, but they do. Help me to expect the best for her always.

Vacation?

*He went up on a mountainside
by himself to pray* (Matt. 14:23).

While I waited for the druggist to fill a prescription, two women, also waiting, talked about their upcoming vacations. One family planned to go to Mexico and the other to Europe.

I would be excited just to have a day off, I thought. One whole day when I didn't have to think about my husband's problems. One day to do only as I pleased. But I don't have vacations. I work 168 hours a week caring for him.

Some days he does so well that I hardly notice the strain. But the roller coaster starts again after a week or a month. So I take mini-vacations by spending an afternoon with friends or going on a three-hour shopping trip. I go for a fast walk or stroll through the park. Each time I come back refreshed and glad for my special kind of vacation.

God, sometimes the best I can do is get away for my mini-vacation. Thanks for providing that for me.

Letting Go

"He can't live here." The doctor did not say "with you," but I felt the sting of the implication that we aren't a proper family. I saw my son's need to live elsewhere as evidence of my failure. I had let him down. No one actually accused me, but they didn't need to. I lived with self-accusations.

Three times my son had come home from the hospital and returned within weeks. I wanted him to get better, and I never consciously thwarted his progress. Yet our personalities are such that we made each other miserable.

If he is to improve, he will have to move into a kind of halfway house and from there on to independent living—all of this away from me.

While I outwardly agreed, inwardly I had not let go. I hurt because I felt self-accused. It took days of internal struggle before I said truthfully, "I want what's best for him." Then I let go.

God, he needs help, and yet I keep thinking mostly about my failure. Forgive me. Thank You for helping me let go.

Burnout

If the tears hadn't welled up, I might have laughed. The primary caseworker for our son resigned recently because of burnout. "Forty to fifty hours a week of pouring my soul out for these hurting people," she said. "I couldn't handle it anymore."

After she left, in a moment of fantasy I thought of resigning as the caring parent. *I'm burned out,* I imagined saying to my son, *and I can't cope with you anymore.* Then reality hit again. I *can't* quit—and even though I occasionally want to, deep inside I know I could never leave him. He needs me. I suppose that's what keeps me away from total burnout.

I read once that all of us need to be needed. I get exhausted and overextended, but there's no giving up as long as he needs my love and my help.

God, You're always there for me, and You've given me a support group to lean on. Give me what I need to be always there for him.

Spiritual Failure

The doctor told her, "You'll probably be on an antidepressant-antianxiety medication like Sinequan for a long time—possibly for the rest of your life."

At home she sobbed a long time. "I'm a spiritual failure. I always had faith in God and believed that God could do anything. But now—"

I held her, trying to comfort her in her pain and confusion. She's not a spiritual failure, and I hope that one day she'll grasp that taking medicine means getting help, not failing—the way she would take medicine for a heart condition.

I want to reassure her, but right now my words seem meaningless. In time I hope she'll see that Sinequan helps her to function each day.

God, thank You for providing medicine for our needs. Teach her and all others who require this kind of help that such drugs are Your gifts to us.

TWO

Clarifying the Focus

Self–Attitude

"I'm no good," my husband muttered. "I can't work. I can't do anything for anybody." The words accompanied his neglect of his personal appearance.

As I prayed for wisdom in knowing what to say, a thought came to me: *Because he doesn't feel good about who he is, he doesn't care how he looks.* A second thought followed: *If he looked better on the outside, he'd feel better on the inside.* I gently insisted that he bathe, shave, and wear clean clothes. I frequently told him how nice he looked, pausing to touch or kiss him.

His improved appearance did pick up his spirits.

He had such low feelings of self-esteem that by being dirty, he was trying to let me know how he really felt. I didn't cure him, but I helped him take care of his body, which enabled him to feel better about himself.

Holy God, I don't know if cleanliness is next to godliness, but I do know that when he's clean he feels better. Let us see his continued improvement.

Perfect Daughter

She was our perfect daughter—attractive, bright, athletic, well groomed, and popular. Her grades hovered at the top of the class. It took her suicide attempt to wake us up.

"But why did you do this?" I pleaded.

After days of sullen silence, she said in a tiny voice, "I got tired of trying to be perfect."

She recounted the history of the demands she believed we had placed on her to surpass everyone. Even when she achieved, it wasn't good enough. She still felt pushed.

"I had no idea," I said limply. For several days I went through a time of self-examination. It did little good to say, "I didn't mean to be that way." I had wanted her to be the best. But I tried too hard. When we talked again, I said, "Forgive me. From now on, I only want you to be happy and to be nobody but the real you—however imperfect you are."

Wondrous God, You allowed me to become authentic. Help me allow her the same opportunity.

"I Hate You"

My son went into tantrums over little things and screamed obscenities at me. The worst came when he said calmly, "I hate you. You have ruined my life." To prevent my bursting into tears, I left the room.

A member of my support group suggested, "He may not mean what he said. He's probably saying he's frustrated. Or that he hates you for that one minute—not always."

"Or," said another, "maybe he's not been able to say things like that before; his language may be an emotional release."

When he now says, "I hate you," I react differently.

"I'm sorry you feel that way," I respond. I touch his hand or kiss his cheek. I want him to know that he can say those words to me and nothing will make me love him less. His freedom to express negative emotions may be necessary before he can articulate positive feelings toward me and others.

God, he's free to say what he feels even when I don't always like the words. Help me to accept him *even when I reject* what he says.

"It's Your Fault"

"I've cut my wrists," she said after having called me out of an important meeting, "and it's all your fault."

She repeated all the ways I had failed her for the last seven years. Such tactics had brought me racing home times before. This time I stayed at work. I said, "I hope you won't kill yourself; I love you."

She interrupted with fresh accusations and again added, "It's your fault."

"No, it's not my fault," I said, surprised at my own calmness. "I won't accept that responsibility." She had used this tactic before. She did not want to die; she needed reassurance of my concern. She also needed to accept responsibility for her own actions.

After hanging up, I wondered if I had done the right thing. What if she *did* take her life? When I got home five hours later, I saw plastic tape over a tiny cut in each wrist. She hasn't threatened to take her life again since then, and I know I did the right thing.

Thank You, God, for giving me the strength to do what's right. We're both better now.

Resentment

Love one another deeply, from the heart (1 Pet. 1:22).

Unwisely I allowed him to alternate sleeping from 12 hours at a time to 2. I ignored his angry outbursts and tolerated his talking jags. And somehow he got better—despite my foolish mistakes. When he came home from the hospital the second time, he said, "I want you to know that I'm holding a lot of resentment against you. You let me stay out of control."

My mistake had been lack of wisdom and insensitivity to his needs.

"I was sick," he said. "I couldn't do anything to stop myself, and I expected your help. I resented your not stopping me."

He has since enabled me to see the importance of my role as caregiver. I promised that if he ever went through phases like that again, I would lovingly intervene. I can help him more by not allowing bizarre behavior.

God, I failed, and I'm sorry. He's forgiven me. Help me not to fail again when he needs me.

Going Backward

Always a meticulous person, she changed drastically. She became unkempt, wore the same clothes for days, and wouldn't bathe or brush her teeth. Then gradually she pulled out of her depression. But a year later she again started to neglect her personal hygiene.

"Have you thought," asked a friend who was caregiver for a 40-year-old son, "that because of internal stress and confusion, she's regressing to an earlier stage in life when someone else took care of her—a time of security?"

His words made sense and helped me to cope better. Without demanding, I ran her bath and escorted her to the tub. While she washed, I laid out fresh clothes. I handed her a comb, and she fixed her hair. Placing the toothpaste and brush on the washbasin was usually all it took for her to brush her teeth.

When she goes through a regressive period, I now know a little better how to cope.

Parent God, make me more sensitive to her needs and more understanding of her regressions.

The Cause

He slept only two or three hours at a time; he moved constantly and talked incessantly. At 3:00 A.M. he decided to repair the back steps. I kept silent, ignoring his strangeness, determined to stay calm. Eventually my anger exploded. "You may get a lot of pleasure out of never sleeping and all this moving around, but I can't stand anymore. Stop doing it!"

I'll never forget his pained expression. "I wouldn't do it if I could stop," he said.

I had gotten so upset over the action that I never thought of the cause.

"We'll work it out together," I said. And we *are* finding ways, because I can now look at the symptoms and not the actions.

God, I'm thankful that You always know what's in my heart and don't judge me on the basis of my actions. Help me to do the same for him.

Hyperactivity

Before she went to the hospital, she didn't want to do anything but sleep. She stayed in bed 16 hours at a time. When she came back, she didn't want to sleep. After 2 or 3 hours she seemed charged up and filled with energy. She wore me out. She started on talking jags, rambling from one topic to another. Or she paced the house, as if she had to be on the move every moment.

I took it as long as I could, and then I called my sister to come over. I had to get away from her or crack up myself. I know that telling her to stop pacing and be calm and sit quietly won't stop her hyperactivity. She can't help doing what she's doing.

Her doctor says that eventually she will settle down and won't be so hyper all the time. As long as she'll pull out of it eventually, I can put up with it—or get someone else to come in when I can't.

God, remind me that her hyperactivity is normal behavior for her in this period of her life.

Oppressive Silence

When he came home from the hospital, he wouldn't speak except to say yes or no. I coaxed, cajoled, and tried to trick him into talking, but he remained adamant. He wouldn't (or couldn't) tell me why. I had never realized until then the oppressiveness of silence. He didn't want the television set on and wouldn't let me play the stereo.

The doctor allayed my worries: "If he doesn't want to talk, respect that right. He'll talk when he's ready or when he has something to say. You go ahead and live your life."

Once in a while he'll talk for a few minutes or an hour. Then silence will prevail for days. But I'm more comfortable with it now, and I no longer find his silence oppressive.

God, I don't enjoy the noiselessness, but at least I can tolerate it. Help me to respect his need for silence.

Depressive Feelings

If any of you lacks wisdom, he should ask God,
who gives generously to all without finding fault,
and it will be given to him (James 1:5).

I'd always heard, "Let people talk about their feelings. Help them get everything out." In her case, it didn't help. She was depressed, and the more she talked about it, the deeper she sank. "I'm no good to you or anybody—I want to die," she would repeat.

When I discussed it with the doctor, he said, "Concentrate on facts and everyday events. Don't deny feelings, but don't dwell on them. She's been carrying around an overload of feelings and needs to get away from them for a while. Let her."

He gave me sound advice. I concentrated on making her comfortable and focused on daily events. Weeks went by before she said, "I still feel awful, but I don't want to die anymore."

That was the first concrete encouragement I had from her. Now I know I must learn when to urge her to talk about feelings and when to avoid such talk.

God, thank You for giving me wisdom through the therapist. Help me to remain sensitive to her needs.

Threats

"Once in a while she gets stubborn, we argue, and then she makes threats."

"What kind of threats?" the doctor asked.

"That she'll do away with herself. That she'll leave the house and never come back."

"Don't take her threats lightly," he said. "At the same time, you don't help any by letting her manipulate you."

After helping me to understand how my daughter played on my fears, the doctor suggested ways for me to respond.

Yesterday my daughter didn't want to take her medicine. "I'll get a lot of pills," she threatened, "and swallow all of them at one time, and then I'll die."

"You need these two tablets," I said. "I'd like you to take them. When you make threats, you scare me, and I wish you wouldn't do that. But threats or no threats, you need these pills." She took them with no further resistance.

Loving God, her manipulative threats still scare me. Give me wisdom to cope with these bad moments.

THREE

Others in Focus

Network Therapy

We developed network therapy from a series of three meetings. It worked like this: We invited everybody who we thought might be of help. This included relatives, former neighbors, my husband's friends from grade school, even his barber. I told them his whole history, not exaggerating and not holding back. They asked questions and spoke of their own feelings and concerns.

At the third meeting we said, "Those who want to help—in any way—here is your chance to volunteer." And they responded.

One man picks him up for church, another brings him home. He has lunch every week with a third person. One man comes over regularly, and they watch vintage films on the VCR. Five others formed a crisis team—people who are available for emergencies. These friends have stood by him for more than two years. He has not had a serious setback since he began the network therapy.

God, thank You for a therapy network—Your hands reaching out to help.

Family Doctors

I have no medical degree, but in many ways I have become his doctor—and so has the whole family. We're not unusual. About 65 percent of mental patients now return to their families, usually their parents. And we have to learn to cope with him and his problems.

And we did learn! Sometimes we make mistakes. We wonder about our own mental health. But we do what we can. We're a family, and we provide the nursing and social network.

"How do you do it?" a friend asked. "The demands on your life seem so great."

"I don't know," I answered truthfully, "but I turn to God for strength and the rest of the family for encouragement. My reward comes when I see our son's smile or when he goes to sleep at night, contented and peaceful."

God, friends tell me I do so much; I thank You for what I can do. I love him, and I know Your parental heart understands.

Something Special

The Lord is full of compassion and mercy. (James 5:11).

When I was growing up, our neighbors had a retarded baby who never learned to walk or talk. I used to feel sorry for them, and one day I told the mother about my concern.

"Thank you," she said. "Some days are hard." Her eyes filled with tears as she added, "But we also have something special. Our little Patty has brought a love into our home that we would never have known otherwise."

I didn't understand her then; now I have had the same experience. Our daughter is 21, and she is mentally ill. Her condition demands so much time and energy that some nights I fall across the bed too tired to undress.

Some days are hard. Yet, like that mother, I know our daughter has brought something special into our home: a deeper compassion for hurting people, a greater sensitivity to needs.

God, despite all the hardship, thank You for giving her to us as a special gift.

Double Trouble

Many people don't understand the double effect mental illness or depression has on the family.

First, the emotional drain: We must constantly watch over him, doing what we can, trying to relieve stress and to express our loving care. That means a constant drain of energy, and sometimes we barely hold on.

Second, the financial drain: They diagnosed my husband as schizophrenic when he was 23, and he's now 31. Despite a good income, we're heavily in debt and envision no future relief.

"How do you handle it?" a friend asked. "I could handle either the sickness or the financial stress, but I couldn't do both."

"You handle what you have to," I said. "I didn't choose this way of life, but I do have a network of friends, sympathetic doctors, and a faith in God that keeps me going."

God, what would I do without You and the helping people You send into my life? Thank You for Your strength.

Not Alone

Aside from her illness, coping with being alone has proven to be the hardest thing I face. For a long time I didn't know anyone else who cared for a mentally ill family member.

Periodically, self-pity struck, and I would hear myself saying, "I can't talk to other people, because nobody else understands what I go through."

In the hospital waiting room I met another man my age, also a caregiver. But he had outside support. He told me about NAMI—the National Alliance for the Mentally Ill—and two other organizations: Emotions Anonymous, and Recovery, Inc.* That week I joined a support group, and for the first time I'm with others who have also experienced pain, loss, shame, and guilt. They understand me and have given me comfort, support, and friendship.

God, I'm never alone with You in my life, and yet I felt that way. Thank You for these groups of people who care.

---

*See a list of addresses at the back of this book.

Draining Off

"Have you drained off your feelings?" a friend asked. "You have to deal with *you* before you can deal with *her* again."

I didn't understand, but he wouldn't let me go until I did.

"'Draining off' means going through each incident that caused you pain. Talk about your hurt with someone you trust. Let the anger, or whatever feelings you have, spill out. Otherwise your emotions remain like a volcano ready to explode."

Right then he let me drain off on him. I admitted my anger, my pain, my embarrassment, my sorrow, and all the other held-back emotions. I didn't totally calm the tumult, but I made a start. By talking in a safe environment and allowing my raw emotions to emerge, I drained them of their power.

God, I've drained off my pain. Now help me rebuild my life while she's getting better.

The Safe Place

Between his constant dependence on me and the children's having different needs for me to respond to, I felt trapped. I had to be strong for everybody.

And I was strong for 10 months, not giving way to tears or allowing myself to get discouraged.

But last week in our self-help group, I couldn't keep it up; I broke down and wept. I couldn't hold back the tears, even though I tried. The group propped me up emotionally and gave me the compassion I needed.

When I tried to apologize for my tears, one of them said, "This is the place to cry or yell or whatever you need to do. We provide a safe place for you here. This is the safe place for all of us. You don't need to apologize, and we hope you'll overcome your embarrassment."

God, thank You for my safe place with those special people who care. They reflect Your compassion for me.

FOUR

Focus on Caring

Promise Little

She did what she could (Mark 14:8).

She was better, and I wanted her to get completely well. I was ready to do anything I could to help. I talked with her doctor, who gave me sage advice: "Promise little; do much."

Later, one of her friends assured me, "I'll drop in to see her every week."

"Don't promise," I said. "Visit, but don't feel guilty if you can't come."

The friend came faithfully for several weeks before she skipped a week—then two weeks. Three months have passed since her last visit. My wife misses her friend's visits, and so do I. But I'm glad I wouldn't let her friend make a promise—and then break it.

I've also stopped myself from overpromising. I want to reassure her, to be available when needed, but I refuse to overcommit. In the long run that's better for both of us.

God, You're the only one whose promises never fail. Thank You that we can rely on Your faithfulness. Strengthen me so that I truly promise little but do much.

Involuntary Commitment

Our son progressed well for 18 months. Slowly the old symptoms started to reappear. We warned him and urged him to get help. "I'm doing fine," he always said.

But he *wasn't* fine; the bizarre behavior patterns recurred. Our only recourse was involuntary commitment. In our state we had to go to court and explain to the judge about his psychotic relapse and his refusal to acknowledge his condition.

We felt grossly humiliated by the entire courtroom scene. Among strangers, we had to prove that he posed a danger to himself and to others and needed temporary hospitalization. In telling of his dangerous behavior, we felt the stigma of shame as if we had caused or exacerbated his problems.

We won in court—or did we? The decision affects us as deeply as it does our son.

God, we, too, have been involuntarily committed, and this realization hurts; we feel alone in our pain. Bring us the comfort and peace that only You can provide.

One Word

I left the hospital in a state of rage. They had her so medicated that she hardly made sense when she tried to talk. One word came to me: *zombie*.

The next day I demanded a meeting with her doctor. "I want you to cut out all that medicine that keeps her doped up." He listened patiently and then summarized her condition with one word that made me reconsider: *overwhelmed*.

"I'd like you to remember it," he said. "That word expresses her emotional state right now. She has had such a flood of emotions that the impact crushed her. We sedated her heavily—temporarily—to give her time and to help pull her out from under the overwhelming load. For right now that level of medication is necessary."

"I never thought of it like that," I said.

God, I still don't like seeing her in a drugged state. Help me to understand that, for now, *she needs to get away from those problems and emotions.*

PPD

"Some patients suffer from PPD—post-psychotic depression—after they return home," his new doctor cautioned after the third hospitalization. "Be aware, and be understanding."

After his first two hospitalizations—both lasting several weeks—we didn't understand PPD and weren't as helpful as we might have been. When he started to show signs of depression, we pushed the panic button. We did not consider that his depressive response might be quite normal.

This time, within a month after coming home, he went into depression. We showered him with extra attention, reminding him that he could go back to the hospital if he needed to. Slowly he pulled out of the despondency.

We hope he won't need hospitalization again, but we've learned to watch for PPD—and to be there with loving assurance and great patience.

God, some of us learn slowly. But thank You that we do learn.

When we heard the proper term, *electric convulsive therapy,* we quickly translated that to *shock treatment* and felt scared. We had heard too many horror stories and seen too many depictions on television programs. Her doctor eased our concern by making several points:

- ECT is used only with selected patients.
- ECT is most effective on people 45 to 55 with no previous history of depression.
- Patients have a minimal (usually temporary) loss of memory.
- Patients tend to sleep deeply afterward.

She had been sleeping fitfully; she dwelt constantly on the past. Because she was a carefully screened patient, the ECT treatment brought an immediate improvement.

God, we get scared about terms and types of treatment. Give us courage and wisdom as we explore the ways that will best help her and others in need.

Did I?

He's been taking an antipsychotic drug with the brand name of Thorazine. About a month lapsed before we saw much change, but since then he has continued to improve.

He is so aware of his dependence on Thorazine that it creates one problem for him. "Did I take it today?" I've heard him ask himself. "I can't remember."

When not sure, he tended to take another, and that could lead to overdosing. Because many of these drugs are cumulative, patients often feel no effect from missing one or two days.

When I realized how deeply this troubled him, I bought a plastic pillbox with a compartment for each day of the week, clearly labeled. Each Sunday he fills the box for the week. If the space for Tuesday is empty, he knows he has taken the pill.

"That relieves my anxiety," he said, "although I sometimes have to check it two or three times a day to make sure."

God, thank You for simple solutions to the problems that plague us each day.

Hospital-Free

I will fear no evil, for you are with me (Ps. 23:4).

The news excited me, and when I told her she said, "Oh, that's fine," although her voice lacked enthusiasm.

My wife had gone through a severe and prolonged depression and voluntarily admitted herself for treatment. After seven weeks, she became an outpatient, going back to the hospital every day for medicine and therapy. As she continued to improve, they cut her return trips to four days a week, then to three, and finally to just one day. Then came the good news: she would not have to return.

She was home two days before I grasped why she took the news badly. She believed the doctor no longer wanted to treat her. She felt abandoned.

"You can go back to the hospital," I assured her, "anytime *you* need to." Now that she understands, she rejoices with me in her successful treatment.

God, so often we misinterpret out of fear and uncertainty. Reassure both of us of Your ongoing presence in our lives.

Convalescence

On the day of his release, we joyfully told him the plans we had made. "We've arranged for you to reenter the spring quarter at college. You have your part-time job back." Two of his friends had arranged welcome-home parties.

"I'd suggest you not make any immediate plans for him," the caseworker said.

"But he's doing better, and—"

"He may not be ready for a lot of activity," she insisted. "If he had undergone major surgery, wouldn't you give him time to recuperate? Think of this in the same way."

We brought him home and put *our* plans on hold. The caseworker was right. He needed to readjust to fit in again. He didn't know if his friends really wanted to see him. For two weeks he stayed inside the house. Then he said, "I want to go to church Sunday." That event began his reentry into the world.

God, thank You for the wisdom You impart to us through others.

Treatment

"Surely you have some kind of drug to cure my husband!" I cited examples of the medical progress in the past 30 years.

"We don't know the cause of mental illness," the doctor said. "Until we do, we can't design the proper drug treatment. At best we hope to control his behavior."

The doctor prescribed lithium carbonate, a drug used since the early 1950s. "It has a powerful mood-stabilizing effect and can be used safely," he said. "Lithium prevents high and low mood extremes."

I wish the doctor had given me a more optimistic picture. My husband's daily lithium doses have caused his manic attacks to occur less frequently, and even when they recur, they're less severe.

While I still hope for a total cure, at least he has relief. Lithium isn't a perfect medicine, but for families like ours, these drugs keep our loved ones functioning.

God, until You give researchers the cure for mental illness, make us thankful for what we have.

Punishing

The testing of your faith develops perseverance (James 1:3).

At first I let him dwell on his self-doubts. He could go on endlessly repeating how bad he was and saying that if I had any brains I would divorce him.

After I learned that I didn't help him by encouraging such self-denigration, I said, "I will not listen to you brood aloud on your failures. You are not a failure."

"If you won't talk about what I want to talk about," he said, "I won't say anything to you." He turned away and refused to speak to me for the rest of that day and for a whole week.

I almost gave in, until I realized he was punishing me for not helping him get worse. I didn't like the silence, and I didn't have to tolerate it. I turned on the TV set. I hummed quietly. One day I read aloud, not sure if he was listening.

He constantly stared at me, anger blazing in his eyes. On the eighth day he spoke to me—only a few sentences, but he had begun.

God, thank You for Your help in winning this battle. I now see that my persistence means we both won.

Rewarding Misery

"I feel so bad, putting you through this," she said. "I've failed you in everything I've ever done. Why do you put up with it? How can you stay with a loser like me?"

For several days I listened, sometimes for hours, while she droned on, recounting every mistake she had made since childhood. Although I didn't recognize the effects of my action then, I was actually rewarding her misery. By letting her focus on self-loathing, I reinforced her words.

At the suggestion of her therapist, I have stopped asking how she feels. I don't give her a chance to parade her misery, because it leads her into deeper despair. Instead, I talk about events and places and people. We're both learning macramé, and we're doing handwork together to give as presents at Christmas.

God, I care deeply about her. I want her to get better, so don't let me reward her misery by listening to all the painful details of failure.

Talking About It

A time to be silent and a time to speak (Eccles. 3:7).

I've always heard that talking about problems makes them easier to handle. I tried the idea out on him. "Just talk to me about how you feel," I pleaded. "Get it out of your system."

"I don't want to," he said.

No matter how hard I tried or how I maneuvered the conversation around to talking about emotions, he wouldn't open up.

In desperation I went to my support group and told them my story. One man said, "Ever try to talk to a drowning person? Talking isn't important then. Saving him is what counts."

Something clicked for me. He doesn't have to talk about how he feels. Instead of helping, I may have hindered his progress. Today I just said, "If you ever get ready to talk about anything, I'll be here."

Wise God, You have a time for all things in life. Help me to respect his right not to talk.

Watching

After she came home, she spent most of the first week in bed. I constantly tiptoed in to check on her. When I went to work, I insisted that she call me every hour. From the time I got home until bedtime, I devoted my attention to her.

But I paid a price. My job suffered. I became irritable. Our relationship deteriorated.

"Why do you keep watching me all the time?" she asked.

"Because I care about you," I said, "and I want to be sure you're all right."

"You're afraid," she said. "You're afraid I'm going to crack up again."

She was right, although I didn't want to admit the truth. She could tell.

"I don't want to go through that again," she said. "But if I do, I won't go off the deep end in two hours. Give yourself a break. Spend a little time caring for yourself."

For once, I took *her* advice!

God, watch over her as only You can. Keep me calmly trusting You.

"Leave Me Alone"

He kept insisting, "Just let me stay by myself." I was reluctant to do that. He had tried to kill himself on two previous occasions—both of them after periods of withdrawal.

He again withdrew from all physical activity. He spent hours staring out the window. He lost interest in conversation. "I'd like to be alone so I can think," he said.

A member of my support group said, "When they're deeply depressed, don't leave them alone. People seldom take their own lives when others are around."

For three weeks I made sure that he was never alone, despite his caustic objections and verbal demands. On his next appointment I told the doctor of my concerns, and she agreed I had done the right thing.

God, sometimes we have to do things we don't like because it's for another person's good. Remind me of that the next time I complain about Your activities in my own life.

Private Space

When our daughter came home after treatment, we were afraid to leave her alone even though she had done nothing violent or self-destructive. We tried to be with her every moment. Someone was available to drive her to and from college or anywhere else.

One day she went on a yelling rampage—one of the first serious signs we had detected before her hospitalization. My heart sank as I thought of the gloomy future.

"Just leave me alone! I am not a puppy you need to keep on a leash," she said.

"What do you want?" I asked, keeping my voice calm.

"I want private space where I can be alone to think things through by myself. You make me feel like a prisoner here."

With reluctance we gave her privacy—exactly what our daughter needed. Her attitude improved, and I soon saw her smiling again.

God, she does need private space. Forgive us for being too protective. Guide us in knowing how to respond lovingly.

A Split Family

My wife left with the final words "I can't take any more." I wish I had understood sooner and gotten more involved. She had stayed home with our daughter. I escaped to my job.

I don't have that option now. I'm what they call the primary caregiver. I had no idea of the continuous strain—emotionally, physically, and financially. Some days I'm ready to quit. I fall asleep at night, hoping I won't have to wake up in the morning.

I wrestle with guilt for not doing more. I still hold some anger toward her mother for running out, even though I understand. I won't run away, but I would like to. I'm here, but it's not always easy.

One thing keeps me going: my daughter needs me, and I love her. Right now she has no one else because we're a split family.

God, I pray that You will unite the three of us again. But even more, I pray that You'll help me be more caring for my daughter and that, as the Great Physician, You will heal her mind.

A Different Husband

I don't like all the changes he's made in the past year! "Just give me back the husband I had—the way he was before he got sick!" I yelled at the doctor. "I don't know what he thinks or how he feels about anything! I knew the other man; this one is a stranger!"

The doctor said, "Maybe you never did know him. You knew the way he behaved but never the real person inside."

I cried that night—and many other nights. I didn't want this supposedly improved husband. I wanted the quiet, agreeable man I had married. Now he gets angry. He wants different food. He says he hates TV. He has made a new circle of friends, and I don't like most of them.

I can't go back to the husband I thought I had before. "I want to love you—the new you—as deeply as I loved the old you," I said. And I meant my words.

God, I still don't want a different husband, but despite what I want, help me to accept the new man—and to do it joyfully.

Being There

I will never leave you nor forsake you (Josh. 1:5).

"Whenever you need to talk, I'm your friend," I promised my daughter. "I'll always be there for you."

A few times she's gone into a rage over simple things I've said. I've listened, but it hasn't been easy. Other times she talks about wanting to die, and I have to restrain myself from pleading, "Don't talk like that."

"The most important thing," the therapist reminded me, "is not to run away emotionally. Be actively present no matter what she says."

Last week I was almost at the end of myself after her screaming obscenities and accusations. Then she paused, smiled, and said, "You know, I can talk to you now. I never could before. Now I know you care."

I left the room glowing inside. I had been available when she needed me. Her recognition makes it easier for me to continue being there.

All-loving God, You never leave me, and that helps me in caring for her. Thank You.

A Parenthesis

Before she got out of the hospital, I worried about how things would be. Our first 10 years of marriage were great. Then she slowly slipped into depressive moods that became more severe. We were practically in divorce court before she agreed to get help.

She's better—better than she's been in a long time. She's also scared.

"I treated you so badly," she said. "I don't want to live like that again."

I explained how I had come to view our life together. "I compared your two years of illness to parentheses in a sentence. When we remove parenthetical expressions, the sentence still makes sense. Let's think about your illness that way—and remove the parentheses."

God, we were so unhappy for so long—but I don't want to remember that. I want to remember the years before she got sick, and I want to concentrate on the years since—beginning with now.

The Memory Jar

Two days before he came home, I made him a memory jar. On small pieces of colored paper I wrote short descriptions of the special times we had shared. I folded the slips of paper and put them inside a clear-glass cookie jar.

I wrote things like "Do you remember when we were so broke we lived for two weeks on nothing but macaroni and cheese? I loved you then. I love you now."

I handed him the memory jar nicely wrapped and said, "Whenever you have a bad day, this is my prescription for you."

He keeps the memory jar by his bed. And he does have bad times. That's when he pulls out a slip of paper and reads it. I can't provide a cure, but the memory jar is one of the things I can do to keep assuring him of my love and presence.

God, I often pause and reflect on how You've been with me through so many of the hard places. Make his memories as helpful to him as mine have been to me.

Remembering

I determined to put the past behind me, but I constantly remembered her mercurial moods. Unconsciously, I expected her to repeat the old patterns of behavior. When she occasionally reverted, I would think, *You haven't changed. You're still the same.*

Yet she *had* changed. I seldom saw the difference, because I concentrated on remembering the past; she focused on the present.

Because I had trouble forgetting what went on during her worst days before she got help, I ignored the healthier woman of today. Quite slowly I recognized the change in her. I could finally say, "For a long time I remembered too much; now I want to forget the past. You're different. You've grown, and I'm beginning to like the changes."

God, at times she has a far healthier attitude than I do. As she continues to grow as a person, help me live better by forgetting the problems of the past. I always want to be thankful for the present.

FIVE

Final Focus

Relapse

I didn't want to consider that he might relapse.

"It's always possible," said the leader of our support group. "Nobody wants it to happen, but it does."

She pointed out signs to watch for in any kind of mental illness:

- Return of the original symptoms
- Staying in bed for long periods
- Lack of response to people
- Strange behavior, such as barricading oneself in a room
- Threatening violence
- Talking nonsense

I've learned from these friends that when relapses occur, I don't have to be devastated. They also assured me that a relapse doesn't mean a complete undoing of all the good. One of them said, "Treat him like a recovering alcoholic who falls off the wagon. He wants to get back on the wagon, so help him."

God, I ask You not to allow him to relapse. But if he does, give me wisdom and strength to handle the situation.

Long Recovery

*The hardworking farmer should be the
first to receive a share of the crops* (2 Tim. 2:6).

Despite the doctor's saying, "He can go home," I insisted that he stay longer. I believed that if he stayed long enough in the hospital, he would get completely well. When he came home the other two times, he had improved and then lapsed into depression and erratic behavior.

"Staying longer won't cure him," she said. "It may make him worse. It's too easy for him now, because he faces no challenges and has no responsibilities."

I had trouble accepting that. But after I brought him home, he said, "I wanted to stay and never come home, because it's safe there, and I didn't have to think or do anything except take my medicine."

The doctor knew; so did my husband. I was the slow learner.

Wise God, remind me that when life gets too easy, we may be preparing for greater hardship. Push us back into action again.

Fearful Feelings

When my daughter first mentioned suicide, I said, "Miserable as life is, it beats the alternative."

Her words scared me, but I did nothing, because I didn't want to think about her death. Then she tried to kill herself. During her hospitalization, I visited for long periods every day, even though her talk about suicide upset me.

The caseworker said, "Be thankful she talks to you about her feelings. That's healthier than holding them inside."

"But I don't want to hear all that."

"Are you afraid? Haven't you ever had feelings like that?"

As a teenager I *had* experienced similar feelings. My daughter was reminding me of what I considered unacceptable. I didn't want to listen, because she stirred up fears and memories of my own suicidal thoughts.

God of courage, help me to accept my fearful feelings. Don't let me shut her off when she expresses emotions that bother me.

The Promise

Our son has his own apartment and a job as part of his independent living therapy. We're allowed to visit and talk to him as much as we like.

One weekend he seemed emotionally low—the worst I had observed since his treatment.

"What's the use?" he asked. "I'm always going to be like this."

Despite our assurances he said, "Maybe I'd better end it all."

Hearing those words brought terror to my heart. I couldn't guard him every minute, so I said, "Make me one promise. If you decide to take your life, call me before you do. Promise?"

After a lengthy discussion, he promised. Recently, months afterward, he said, "My dumb promise is what kept me from killing myself that weekend."

Friends in my support group have extracted similar promises from their family members, too, in such crises. And it works.

Lord, I've promised to love and help him. Your never-failing promises of help comfort me.

Until

Our daughter said, "The world will be a better place without me."

I debated whether my wife and I ought to try to talk her out of any suicide attempt, but we knew she would resent our efforts.

Finally my wife said, "Problems often look worse at night. If we put off hard decisions until morning, life looks different in the sunshine." She kissed our daughter and said, "Promise me you won't make any drastic decision until morning."

A lengthy discussion followed, but she did promise. When we left, she said, "Until morning," and closed the door.

We spent a troubled night, but she phoned us the next morning, "I'm going back to the hospital," she said. "I didn't sleep. Only one word kept me from hurting myself." It was the word *until*. "It gave me something to live for—if only for a few hours. Now I know I want to keep on living."

Lord, thank You for until, *because it offers us hope and peace.*

Call the Expert

When my husband talked about taking his life, he scared me, and I didn't know what to do. At first I tried to joke with him and get his mind off the topic. It didn't work.

Then I called his doctor. I apologized for phoning, but the doctor said, "This is the time you need to call."

I accompanied my husband to the doctor's office the next day. After checking him over, she increased his antidepressant medication.

"If he talks about suicide again—or even hints of it—you are to call me, night or day," the doctor said to me privately.

The doctor doesn't know how much she comforted me. Now I know that if the situation arises again, I have assistance readily available.

God, You are always ready to aid us, and usually through people. I forget so easily. Forgive me.

Lethal Weapons

We've never had guns in our house, so when I heard members of my support group talk about keeping lethal weapons away from the patients, I paid little attention.

Then one evening she jabbed herself in the stomach twice with scissors before I could stop her. Fortunately, she made only superficial wounds. But from then on, I seriously considered every possible lethal weapon in the house.

She had disposable razors, and I discovered a letter opener and four sharp knives—all lethal.

To hide things only meant that she would play detective when I was out of her sight. I placed potential weapons in places where she would not automatically see them. Seeing could lead to using.

If she decides to take her life, I may not be able to stop her, but I want to take all possible preventive measures.

God, give her such a desire for life that she'll forget about death. Help me to encourage that desire.

Coded Messages

He had long since stopped talking about suicide, and we felt relieved. But one day a statement disturbed me—as if he was giving us a message in code. I detected something wrong, not in the words but in the subtle voice change. "That barking dog next door won't trouble me anymore." I hoped he didn't plan to kill the dog, which often awakened us in the middle of the night.

After a few more coded statements, I realized that he was planning to take his own life. I contacted his therapist, who told me two things: First, he probably was giving me a coded message not only of intent but also of a plea for help. Second, "He's serious, so watch him carefully."

We kept him from carrying out his self-destructive plans. Now that we've passed that crisis, I've come to understand him better and to listen for coded messages.

God, You understand my unclear messages. Enable me to understand his.

Hoarding

*Let us draw near to God with a sincere heart
in full assurance of faith* (Heb. 10:22).

Quite accidentally I found her supply of pills. One word flashed into my mind: *suicide.* She's hoarding the pills until she has enough to take her life.

I kept watching her behavior and saw nothing to indicate that she was thinking that way. Yet I had the evidence. I finally confronted her with the cache.

"I *have* been hoarding them," she said sheepishly. "I sneak one or two out of every bottle—just a few so you won't notice. I know I need this medicine to keep on getting better. I've been afraid that something might happen and the doctor would cut me off. If he did, I figured I'd still have enough to last me for months—in case."

With the doctor's cooperation, I keep an unopened bottle of pills in the house. The presence of the bottle assures her that, no matter what, she will have all the medicine she needs.

Lord, I suppose at times we all need a little extra assurance. Give it to her now.

Afterward

Next year we'll both be 70, and our son will be 43. According to all the statistics, he will outlive us. Then what happens?

We're deeply concerned, and as his parents, we've discussed the subject often enough. He is not able to care for himself or go into an independent living situation. He needs someone.

We have no other children. A few governmental programs now provide for people like him. But we still worry. We're actively involved in setting up community services, but people are slow to respond, especially when we propose tax increases. They give research grants for cancer and AIDS—and they should—but when it comes to mental illness, we seem way down the list. And we worry.

God, as long as we're alive and able, he will have the loving care he needs. But what happens afterward? Assure us, please, that he will be cared for.

Reunion

I had not seen her for 23 months. I told everyone I did not want to see her again or even to think about her. She was not only mentally unbalanced—she had tried to kill me.

A chaplain at the hospital contacted me and begged me to visit. "Your presence could greatly affect her improvement."

Reluctantly I agreed to visit "for a few minutes."

When I saw her, something happened inside me. Impulsively I embraced her and heard myself say, "I love you, and I forgive you."

Until that moment I hated her and never wanted to see her again. But on seeing her again, a miracle took place—the rekindling of my love. A month after my visit, she came home for the weekend. If she continues to improve, she'll soon be well enough to live at home.

I'm surprised again, but now I want her home—with me.

God, thank You for rekindling my love. Forgive me for my neglect.

Tomorrow?

Today was a wonderful time. Everything went right all day. Perfect weather. Happy mood. No stress. He behaved so well that no observer would ever have known of his mental illness.

Today was wonderful. I allowed myself to enjoy each experience. That's how I cope with life. I can't presume about tomorrow; I don't even want to think about tomorrow. I survive emotionally by being thankful for the present.

I used to devote so much energy toward preparing myself for the unknown. I would have said to myself, *Yesterday he behaved as well as he did today. But tomorrow?*

People like us, caregivers, have no guarantees about the future. We have no tomorrow—only today.

God, thank You for the comforting words "Do not worry about tomorrow; it will have enough worries of its own. There is no need to add to the troubles each day brings" (Matt. 6:34, TEV). *Because You're with us.*

Out of the Closet

As parents, family members, and friends, we're proud of ourselves. We love and provide care for mentally sick individuals. We're present when they need us.

In the beginning, we didn't talk outside our family about the mentally ill person. But now some of us have come "out of the closet." We tell other people, because we have nothing to be ashamed of. Many of us have become activists for the cause of the mentally ill. We're not hiding our loved ones in sealed-off institutions. We're telling our stories and asking people to help us. They can assist through political involvement and legislative pressure. We urge corporations to provide grants for further study. And we realize that not only does this activism help our loved ones— it also gives us a deep sense of satisfaction.

God, I want to be able to say at the end of my life, "I did what I could." With Your encouraging support, I can do that.

Additional Resources

Support Organizations

Emotions Anonymous, P.O. Box 4245, St. Paul, MN 55104.

National Alliance for the Mentally Ill, 1901 North Fort Myer Drive, Suite 500, Arlington, VA 22209.

Recovery, Inc., 116 South Michigan Ave., Chicago, IL 60003.

Recommended Reading

Newsletters and pamphlets

NAMI *Newsletter,* published bimonthly by National Alliance for the Mentally Ill.

U. S. Department of Health and Human Services. *Medicine for the Layman: Depression and Manic Depressive Illness.* 1982.

U. S. Department of Health and Human Services. National Institute of Mental Health. *Depressive Disorders: Causes and Treatment.* 1983.

Books

Bennett, George. *When the Mental Patient Comes Home.* Christian Care Books. Philadelphia: Westminster Press, 1980.

Hatfield, Agnes B. *Coping with Mental Illness in the Family: A Family Guide.* Arlington, Va.: NAMI, 1984.

Torrey, E. Fuller. *Surviving Schizophrenia: A Family Manual.* New York: Harper and Row, 1983.